I0455565

# STAND UP AMERICA

By

## DR. HAROLD B. HUBBARD

Order this book online at www.trafford.com
or email orders@trafford.com

Most Trafford titles are also available at major online book retailers.

© Copyright 2010 Dr. Harold B. Hubbard.
All rights reserved. No part of this publication may be reproduced, stored in a retrieval system, or transmitted, in any form or by any means, electronic, mechanical, photocopying, recording, or otherwise, without the written prior permission of the author.

Printed in the United States of America.

ISBN: 978-1-4269-3677-7(sc)
ISBN: 978-1-4269-4315-7 (ebk)


*Our mission is to efficiently provide the world's finest, most comprehensive book publishing service, enabling every author to experience success. To find out how to publish your book, your way, and have it available worldwide, visit us online at www.trafford.com*

*Trafford rev. 09/01/2010*

 www.trafford.com

**North America & international**
toll-free: 1 888 232 4444 (USA & Canada)
phone: 250 383 6864 ♦ fax: 812 355 4082

## ACKNOWLEDGEMENT

In no manner could these pages have become a reality without the collaboration and expert editing by Dr. Judith Navarro--Chief/Retired-- Office of Publications, Pan American Health Organization/ World Health Organization, Washington D.C.

# CONTENTS

# PREFACE

It is amazing how the Patriots of the American Revolution sacrificed their lives, how they fought and died to remove the yoke of King George's tyranny from their society, and yet, today , we Americans accept a similar tyranny wielded by the professional politicians of the Federal Government, without as much as a feather of protest to lift it. This book offers the reader and all Americans a description of the principles and an elaboration of the practices needed to reform the Federal Government, so that we can regain control of our lives. The purpose in publishing these pages is to motivate collective thinking, to be followed by concerted actions, that will reverse the trend of government's ever-greater intrusion into individuals' lives and its curtailment of their freedoms. Among other recommendations, it encourages the American people to create once again a representative U.S. Congress by electing to the House of Representatives and the Senate those who will be responsive to the people's needs and their wishes. The book aims to awaken readers to the growing control the Federal Government has over their very existence, and most especially their hard-earned income, with increased spending on programs that for the most part offer no benefit to the average American family, resulting in ballooning deficits, inevitably to be accompanied--with every budget cycle-by higher taxes.

## CHAPTER ONE

"The Buck Stops Here" declared the famous sign that sat on the desk of President Harry S. Truman all of the days he served as President of the United States. In the years that followed, subsequent Presidents from "The Greatest Generation" knew exactly what that sign meant as they did their best to hold true to the principle. Today -- inside of the beltway , within the "Good Ol`Boys Club"--most politicians clearly don`t understand the meaning of this basic premise of accountability.

The Constitution states,"of the prople, by the people and for the people." Yet, today, we the electorate are forced to ask a simple question : "Where is the "for the people" part?" It is past time that we collectively insist on a government that responds to the needs and desires of the populace, one that is wholly constituted by citizen representatives. Achieving such a government will require major reform.

### LEGISLATIVE BODIES

To be responsible and responsive to all Americans, every legislative body at the various levels of government --federal, state, county, and city -- must be completely overhauled. To begin with, no legislature should be allowed to have in its member body more than 15% of lawyers. Where in any democracy is a single profession allowed to write and pass all of the laws that it subsequently utilizes in the propagation and perpetuation of its own profession?

Lawyers in the various government legislatures pass laws that support the efforts of over zealous prosecutors, who then use their thus acquired "authority" to enhance and further their personal political careers. At the federal level, the country would be better served by having some type of commission made up of citizens representing every state, drawn from in respective state legislatures; that commission would convene alternately in different regions of the country. Among its other duties, the commission would assure that the number of lawyers elected to the U.S .Congress never exceeds the 15% permitted; they would remove anyone whose prescience signifies a transgression of that limit and appoint non-lawyers to replace them. This commission should be comprised of men and women who have been selected by a 60% vote from their respective legislatures.

The very same procedure should be followed at the state, county, and local levels of government. The American people deserve better representation than that which they are forced to tolerate today. Ever bigger government populated by members of the legal profession is not representative of the Constitution, much less the people. All voters in the United States of America should stand up today and take back their government, so that it can be responsive to the essential requirements of citizens everyday life.

The television channel C-span does an excellent job of covering the activities of the U.S. Congress. That coverage reveals everyday that the patriotism of our Founding Fathers and many patriots since has been replaced by greed-- both political and financial. A careful review of recent debates in the House of Representatives exposes the abandonment of House rules and the application of censorship of the minority party to demonstrate information that they consider to be pertinent to passage of laws by the majority party simply so it can have its way and because it has the overwhelming number of votes. It is the so-called " Blue Dog Democrats" who have courageously campaigned for the return to a true democratic process.

Almost three centuries ago, a wise history professor from the University of Edinburgh, Alexander Tyler, warned in 1727 that a " democracy will continue to exist up until the time that voters discover that they can vote themselves generous gifts from the public treasury. From that moment on, the majority always votes for the candidates who promise the most benefits from the public treasury , with the result that every democracy will finally collapse due to loose fiscal policy, followed by a dictatorship." The quest for "generous gifts" at the expense of the common wealth has to cease, be ceased or else the U.S. democracy will collapse. It is time the "fuzzy ideas of Foggy Bottom" are blown away from the Washington D.C. scene.

Patriotism starts with the family and is reinforced in the schools at the high school level, where the students are soon to be of age to vote. The Goldwater Institute in Phoenix , Arizona released the results of a survey of high school students in that State. It revealed that  most of those could not pass the required test to become an American citizen. Toward that end, immigrants must answer six of 10 questions, among which are: 1) What is the supreme law of the land? (Constitution); 2) What do you call the first 10 amendments to the Constitution? (The Bill of Rights); 3) What are the two parts of the U.S. Congress?; (Senate and House) 4) How many justices on the the Supreme Court? (Nine); 5) Who was the first President of the United States? (George Washington). Of 1,140 high school students who took this test, only 3.5% answered six of the 10 questions correctly. For this Republic to survive, its citizens should have a basic knowledge of the country's government, history, and geography. What happened to the classes in civics that Americans had to pass in order to graduate from high school? As fathers, many of the members of "The Greatest Generation" taught these patriotic values at the family dinner table! Today, with a large number of families abandoned by their fathers , principally  in urban centers, mothers are forced to assume the inculcation  of civic values; however, this responsibility  becomes just another of too many for them to take on.

## SALARIES OF ELECTED OFFICIALS

Multiple millions of dollars are spent every election on countless political campaigns across the country, yet the sources of these millions remain a great secret, a complete mystery. Most of them come from large corporations, associations, unions, self-interested individuals, political action committees, and other groups all of whom have a sole motive: to receive, in return for their patronage, some benefit or special privilege from the politicians they helped elect.

To avoid these compromises, the amount of monies spent on the election of any individual to any legislative or executive body should be no more than the salary that individual would receive in that position. This should apply at all levels of government, federal, state, county and local. Once instituted, this change in campaign financing will assure that elected officials are dedicated to the service of the full body of their constituents, with no obligations to any particular group or individuals.


## TENURE OF SERVICE

It is time to eliminate professional politicians from the American system of democracy. They feed upon the population like a "horde" of parasites, with no control nor treatment to remove them. ONE term of service is adequate for all politicians! They should leave office during the next elective term, as no consecutive terms should be permitted.

Why is this system of incumbency a problem? Take, for instance, the extended terms of some of our professional politicians in the U.S. Senate who have served until they are in their 90's. While some nonagenerians are more lucid than their younger contemporaries, all of us know of cases of senators whose capacity to serve was greatly compromised by their inability to read, comprehend and respond to the legislative process and who depended almost exclusively on their unelected staff for help. Meanwhile, a much younger person would better serve his or her constituents and the country. One six year term should be adequate for all senators.

One two-year term should be adequate for representatives in the House of Representatives. Furthermore, many American citizens of voting age, with a minimum of two years study at a university, should be considered and requested to serve one term in the House of Representatives. They should be selected by a commission appointed by the state legislature that has predetermined their capacity to serve. Their service should be obligatory, as the military draft used to be.

The U.S. Congress today is a good-ol'-boys club made up of inside the beltway demagogues who carry out the orders of big business, corporations, and a conspiracy of petroleum speculators. An example proves the point:: The Federal Trade Commission (FTC) lawyers could file an antitrust suit against the monopoly held by the oil cartel, but if they were to do so, the U.S. Congress would eliminate the FTC. Why? Simply because that cartel supports the election of Congressmen. Good-ol'-boys club inside the beltway? As stated earlier, it is time to remove the corrupt and self-serving interests with their "fuzzy ideas from the seat of national government.

"America will never be destroyed from the outside. If we falter and lose our freedoms, it will be because we have destroyed ourselves." (Abraham Lincoln)

# CHAPTER TWO

## LOBBYISTS

Today the greatest detriment to effective government for the people of this country, people who pack their lunch, go off to work every day,pay their bills and taxes (however reluctantly), educate their children, and are the salt of the earth Is the poor representation they receive from their elected officials. Lobbying is the biggest activity in the U.S. Congress, as special interests daily impose their damaging influences on the laws of the country. One U.S. Representative , from Colorado, told me that he spent 90% of his time listening to lobbyists, who many times kept him from reporting to the Chamber of the House of Representatives to vote on important legislation.

Lobbyists have only one interest in their relationship with members of the U.S. Congress and that is to peddle their influence on legislation to benefit those who hire them. And, with few exceptions, most of those lobbyists are lawyers! As previously noted, the influence of the legal professsion on legislative bodies and thus on the formulation of our laws is grossly outsized. Their fingerprints are all over every piece of legislation at all levels of government. As quoted by large numbers of lawyers in the political arena ," Absence of evidence is no evidence of absence. " A considerable number of lawyer lobbyists are utilized as consultants or permanent advisors to some members of the U.S. Congress.

We as a nation have forgotten the farewell address of  President George Washington, upon leaving office! There were several important phrases in it.

Two of these phrases are more significant today, 1) " Remember the standards that started the revolution" and 2) "Remember what brought us together". As a apropos to the lobbyists situation today, another phrase in that address is: "Morality in politics is guided by belief in one God".

There is no greater need within the legislative process than to control, restrain, and restrict the influence and subsequent activities of lobbyists. We must regulate the amount of time lobbyists have each week with Congressmen and women, the time of day and the number of visits per month they can make to the offices of the members of Congress. It should also be unlawful to contact or meet with members of Congress outside of their offices, including when members return to their districts to meet with their constituents. A national rationalizing commission should be established, by majority vote of all state legislatures, to regulate, control, and approve the number,consistency, and standards of lobbyists. It might determine the types of activity and interests represented by lobbyists and the year in which the lobbyists might be permitted to function. All lobbyists might be allowed to contact members of Congress only during the year they are approved, and no lobbyist nor their associates may serve two years in a row.Thusly, a lobbyist may contact a member of Congress every other year. Therefore, long-term planning by the commission ensues and allows the American people to prepare for the lobbyists action. It could further be required that the lobbyists submit proposals to the members of Congress six months in advance.

Furthermore, a lobbyist should not be able to serve in that capacity until first having passed a state licensing examination and until being approved by 60% of the vote of the state legislature in which the lobby group resides. Afterward, the national rat ionalizing commission might give its approval to the lobbyist interacting with members of Congress. The lobbyist would then apply to a committee of the House of Representatives that would have the authority to control lobbyists, possibly the House Rules Committee, to request an interview with a specific individual member of Congress. The lobbyist would be permitted only one contact with that member of Congress and would have to solicit approval for any additional meeting with a different member on another occasion. Each year, all state legislatures, with new members, would have to approve a new list of lobbyists that would then be submitted to the national rationalizing commission for consideration. All Americans should return control of the legislative process of this country to the people, who the Constitution originally designated, and away from special interests and their hired lawyers who wish to promote their form of socialism

# THE ELECTIVE PROCESS

Hillary Clinton won the majority of the primary votes, but lost the nomination of the Democratic Party due to the caucus method. John McCain won the majority of the primary votes and won the nomination of the Republican Party for the 2008 presidential election. Yet, neither John McCain nor Hillary Clinton ended up in the White House. Something is seriously wrong with this disparate process. Caucuses are a travesty to the intent, dedication, and hard work of those persons working and voting In these elections. When one considers the benefits versus the detriments of the caucus process, it becomes clear that it should have passed into obscurity 100 years ago. The caucus system is no longer needed and is in fact counterproductive, because it leads to and encourages voting place workers to be dishonest and corrupt. For example, during the elective progression for the nominations of 2008, a group called "ACORN" falsely registered persons who never existed or were long dead; one non-existing person was even registered 87 times. "ACORN" is now under investigation for voter fraud in 14 States while one of its former employees has been elected President of the United States of America. Once again we have the "fox guarding the chicken house"! It is time the "burros" are removed from the "burrocracy" and put honest, dedicated American patriots back in charge of the whole elective course of action.

How does a candidate win all of the caucuses , lose the primaries where the true members of the party actually go to the polls and vote , and up till now win the nomination? It is uncomplicated! The candidate needs only to get started in the nomination design very early--that is before the other candidates enter the race--by placing key personnel at the local level in order to assume persons loyal to him/her are named to the caucuses. Loyalty may be secured in many ways ,but principally it derives from campaign money or political promises, of which many are never kept. When the caucuses vote, it is a done deal and all within the approved electoral practice! Thus did candidate Michael Dukakis win the nomination of the Democratic Party for the presidential election won by Ronald Reagan by a landslide. In reality, he only represented a minority of the Democrats while many of the majority --"Reagan Democrats"-- went on to vote for Ronald Reagan. Given the modern system of electronic communications, the archaic caucus method of selecting a party candidate has no place and cannot be justified. It might have served its purpose when the results had to be carried personally to Washington D.C. Today we know the results within hours, minutes even. The caucus structure is obsolete and should be eliminated, replaced by the primary classification. "You are responsible for your political actions because posterity is those unborn yet" , George Washington`s Farewell Address!

At the same time, the primary classification requires overhauling completely so that all of the states are obligated to have a primary election, moreover, all state primaries should be held within a maximum of 60 days from the first to the last.

## PARTY CONVENTIONS

Among the most outrageous spectacles forced upon the American people every four years are the two political party conventions. Enormous amounts of money are spent , as rhetoric spews forth; proof positive of the fallacy of the caucus process for selecting a candidate to represent each party in the general election. An example of the distortion that results from this course of action is the fact that 46% of the delegates to the 2008 Democratic National Convention were of Hispanic origin--possibly the results of the efforts of ACORN and the caucus process--whereas Hispanics represent a far smaller percentage of the general population.

The time and resources entailed in holding these conventions are ridiculous. This leaves very little time for the campaigns and for the candidates to meet with the electorate and the media who analyzes and comments fully on their respective platforms. Moreover, after the inauguration, almost none of the platform positions are subsequently instituted by the winner, thereby, rendering these conventions purposeless. With the elimination of the caucus method and with timely held primaries, national conventions should be held earlier.

# CHAPTER THREE

## STEALING THE ELECTION

There are two basic ways to steal an election from the American voter.
One is exemplified by which occurred in the presidential election of
November 2000 when the total votes in Florida were compromised by
incompetence of local and state officials and could not be counted. In one
county, 15,000 votes were disenfranchised. That many votes would have given
the election to Al Gore. Consequently, because of interference by the Secretary
of State and the Governor of Florida, who at the time was the brother of the
Republican candidate, the Supreme Court of the United States of America
declared George W. Bush the winner. Significantly, the vote by the Supreme
Court was five in favor of the Republican and four against. Interestingly, the five
Judges voting for George W. Bush were nominated by Republican Presidents
and the four voting against were nominated by Democratic Presidents. The
Supreme Court failed the American electorate shamefully by interfering and
automatically cancelling the votes of millions of Americans. Likewise, the
status and confidence in the Court among Americans dropped enormously.
The Supreme Court intervened in the process of the American politics with
total disregard for their own "razon d`etre".

The other way to steal an election is called the Electoral College.

A candidate requires only 270 votes out of a total of 538 to win an election.

The founding fathers of the Constitution era made a compromise between an

election of the President by the Congress and an election by popular vote,

which led to establishment of the Electoral College. The Electoral College

consists of 538, one for each of 435 members of the House of Representatives

100 Senators and by reason of the 23$^{rd}$ Amendment, 3 from the District of

Columbia. The decennial census is used to reapportion the number of electors

allocated among the States. To no one's surprise, the slate of electors are

generally chosen by the political parties. Moreover, it is equally strange that

our founding fathers , within the Constitution, established the United States of

America as to be for rights of the individual

The electors meet in each State on the first Monday after the second

Wednesday in December following the general election in November.

A majority of 270 votes electoral votes is required to elect the President and

Vice-President. No Constitutional provision or Federal law requires electors to

vote in accordance with the popular vote in their State. If no presidential

candidate wins a majority of electoral votes, the 12$^{th}$ Amendment to the

Constitution provides for the presidential election to be decided by the

House of Representatives by majority vote. Although chosen by the

the political parties, in most States, the electors are appointed by statewide
popular election. The slate of electors for the candidate who receives the most
popular votes is appointed. The question often asked by a vast majority of
American voters is "Why do we still have the Electoral College?" In a survey
In 1981, 28 years ago, 75% of those questioned favored abolishing the
Electoral College. Today one might presume the response would be 90-95%
opposed. The Electoral College, like the caucus system in the primaries, is
antiquated and has outlived its original purpose, which may have been
necessary before the advent of modern means of communication. For example,
there were no telephones at the time of its inception, and the results had to be
hand carried to Washington D.C., whereas today many American voters do not
even have landline telephones in their homes, due to the introduction of the
mobile telephone. It is a travesty and a detriment to those Americans who wish
to vote but think their vote will not count because the election is decided by the
five or six states with the largest populations  The election of November, 2008
Is a prime example. How can  young American voters enjoy the right and
privilege of voting when they think their votes do not count? It has been a huge
blocking force against the formation of an independent ,third political party,
which is desperately  needed on the political scene today. A major segment
of the electorate today considers themselves independent voters and have the
political power to control every election. It is time the Electoral College went by

the way of the horse drawn carriage! Let us get started, "Stand Up America!"

In 1987, the American Bar Association criticized the Electoral College as

"archaic" and "ambiguous", and 69% of its members-over two thirds- favored

abolishing it. Political scientists, however aggressively, supported continuation

of the Electoral College! The "Good `Ol Boys Club" inside the beltway at work

once more.

Any proposal to change the election process, vis-a` vis , the Electoral

College and make a nationwide election by the people would require passage by

the Congress in the form of an amendment to the Constitution with a two-thirds

majority in both houses of Congress and ratification by three-fourths of the

States. Controlling the legislative process in both of these bodies are the

professional politicians with very little inclination to make any change that might

affect the perpetuity of their careers.

The moving force behind the number of electors of the Electoral College is

the census conducted by the U.S. Government every 10 years. What is the

decennial census and how does it affect the number of members of the House

of Representatives?

Another prime example to give the American people reason to eliminate the Electoral College, are the results of a study conducted by Professor Joseph Olson, HAMLINE UNIVERSITY, School of Law , St.. Paul, MN. about election of November, 2008 . A careful review of his report reveals the following:
1) number of States won by the Democrats were 19 whereas the number of States won by the Republicans were 29, 2) square miles of land in the areas won by the Democrats were 580,000, yet won by the Republicans were 2,427, 000, 3) populations of Counties won by the Democrats was 127 million while that won by the Republicans was 143 million, 4) a very significant finding was the homicide rate per 100,000 residents in those Counties won by the Democrats was 13.2 , meanwhile the rate in those Counties won by the Republicans was 2.1.

What does this mean? It signifies that the Democrat won the presidential election by the number of electoral votes from a few States while the rest of the votes from that 143 million Americans did not even count.. Something is seriously wrong with this practice which continues to be a deterrent to the Incentive for the young person to vote.

# DECENNIAL CENSUS

The impact of the decennial census on the process of "stealing the election" Is prevalent in those areas with high concentrations of the population, such as inner cities and their suburbs. Land developers in the suburbs have great Influence on the mobility of families around big cities. Shopping mall construction accompanying the large tracts of houses, and in the process destroys vast areas of natural habitat, affect the movement of these populations, Likewise, the major changes in population documented by the decennial census can prompt local politicians to create additional congressional districts. New districts allow the predominant political party, whether Democrat or Republican, to gain another seat in the House of Representatives of the U.S. Congress.

The official U.S. census as described in the Constitution of the United States calls for an actual enumeration of the people every 10 years which in turn is to be used for apportionment of seats in the House of Representatives among the states. The first official census was conducted in 1790 under Thomas Jefferson, then the Secretary of State . U.S. marshalls on horseback, counted 3.9 million.

After the very first time, the census has been conducted every 10 years, usually on April 1 in years ending in a zero. The census statistics have been used in many ways for other purposes. Consequently, the Census Bureau acquired the enormous responsibility of enumerating small area population figures essential for redrawing state and congressional districts.

Similarly, the information is used for the distribution of government funds among government programs, such as Medicaid, school location planning, other public facilities, and roads. One can imagine the benefits to businesses like real estate offices and to potential residents seeking a new neighborhood. Considerable geographical facts are also obtained on states, counties, cities, towns, ZIP codes, census tracts , and blocks-- all of which are then used by universities on studies of future economics, demographics, research and development. What is asked in the census on its short form?

First is age, followed by sex, ethnicity, household relationship, race, whether the home is owned or rented and vacancy characteristics. The long form is considerably more complicated, with 15 parts related to population and another 11 associated with housing. The Census 2000 also incorporated American Somoa, Guam, the Commonwealth of the Northern Mariana Islands, and the U.S. Virgin Islands. Sets of decennial data available are 1) 110th Congressional District files 2) Census 2000 state Legislative District summary files 3) American Indian Alaska Native Summary and 4) data from the 1990 Decennial Census. It is the driving power behind the metamorphosis of the big cities versus rural America , which is disappearing rapidly through encroach-ment by the huge tracts of houses and associated shopping malls, with subsequent reduction in agriculture production and the requirement to produce more on less land.

# GERRYMANDERING

This political process and political maneuvering evolve directly as a result of the decennial census. Gerrymandering is the drawing of election district boundary lines for partisan advantage to favor majority party and incumbent politicians of all political parties. It is a form of election fraud that misuses redistricting to violate the one voter-one vote fairness principle that redistricting is intended to preserve. Why do many politicians engage in political corruption without concern for subsequent voter anger and rejection at the next election? They represent gerrymandering election districts where voters do not choose their politicians, rather the politicians choose their voters! This is true in gerry-mandering districts throughout the country.

Three techniques are used to gerrymander districts. Each involves creating districts that have a goal of encompassing a certain percentage of voters from one political party. These three techniques are: 1) "excess vote" is an attempt to concentrate the voting power of the opposition into just a few districts, thereby diluting their power: 2) "wasted vote", which uses the strategy of diluting the voting power of the opposition across many districts and , in doing so, prevents the opposition from having a majority; and,3)"stacked method" which involves drawing crazy boundaries to concentrate power of the majority party by linking specific, party-in-power districts. Unconditionally, all these techniques violate the fairness principle of one voter-one vote intended by the Constitution!

A prime example of gerrymandering was the creation of the 7$^{th}$ Congressional District of Arizona. Following the 2000 decennial census and created in time for the 2002 elections, it is larger than Rhode Island, Delaware, Hawaii, Connecticut and New Jersey combined. Arizona had a Democratic Governnor with a Department of Justice appointed by her. The Districting Commission had previously drawn the area into various districts of several different counties. The Department of Justice objected to the existing districts and demanded that the Districting Commission to create the 7$^{th}$ Congressional District. A much larger district with 50.6% residents of Latino-Hispanic origin and the rest principally Native Americans. In the 2002 election voters elected Mr. Raul Grijalva to office with a 59% majority and reelected him in 2004,2006 and 2008.

The district includes 300 miles along the United States border with Mexico. It has become obvious after careful review of the voting record of Rep. Grijalva that amnesty for illegal immigrants crossing the border is one of his priorities. His conduct has illustrated gerrymandering at its most egregious with the Democratic party in the majority at that time. The voters do not choose the politicians--the politicians choose the voters. His election constitutes fraud against the one voter-one vote fairness principle. It appears that if ACORN, with their voter registration frauds cannot achieve this redistricting of geographical representation then the gerrymandering politician will --all within the law. Yet, it is worth bearing in mind once again the fundamental tenet of the Constitution: "of the people, by the people and for the people"

# CHAPTER FOUR

## ELECTION POLLS AND THE MEDIA

Many months before November 8, 2008, the American people were saturated ad nauseum with the coverage of the upcoming election by the media and their election polls. Is it any wonder that a considerable number of qualified American voters refused to go to the voting polls on election day? They were sick to death and grievously angered at the media through their coverage of the two political parties, including their attacks on personal aspects of the candidates and their families. Election polls and accompanying results were the engines that incited the media procedures.

Unscrupulous, unprincipled coverage of the lives of the family of Sarah Palin, duly elected Governor of the State of Alaska and Vice-Presidential candidate of the Republican Party, drew the ire and outrage of the American public. Their malicious but cruel attacks on the daughter of Sarah Palin, along with her fiance, produced animosity against the vicious liberal press such as the New York Times, ABC, CBS, NBC, and CNN who at the time endorsed the candidate of the Democratic Party. Election polls also had a colossal impact on those voters who voted by mail and absentee ballot. Furthermore, the media coverage of the complete meltdown of the financial world in mid-September and the liberal analysis that centered the blame on the Bush Administration Impacted election polls to the point that it decisively guaranteed the path to the White House for Barack Obama.

# EXIT POLLS

Most Americans had their eyes glued on the news from the national media through the major television networks on election night of November 8, 2008. Each channel was offering the latest voting information through its own reporting system identified as part of its own network. Wrong! Using maps, charts, tables, geographical locations as if all originated within the networks such as ABC, CBS, NBC, CNN and FOX. Every one of these networks had previously contracted private agencies that were feeding the exit-poll information to the networks through an electronic service. Some were reliable, but many were simply based upon hearsay. Should the public rely on and put its trust in exit polls? Absolutely not! Demonstrable were the results emanating from the exit polls in the evening of the 2004 national elections, which illustrated that those polls leaning toward Senator John Kerry made it look like President Bush was being defeated at 5 pm.. In reality, it did not turn out like that, as everyone now knows. The quandary associated with this false reporting is that many voting polls in the western United States are still open at the time the polls close in the eastern USA yet the information that is reported greatly influences the mental status of those voters who have not voted and do not wish to vote for a loser. A large percentage of those agencies providing exit polls information to the television networks have no idea what they are talking about nor reporting. It is a system that affects the total votes and the Electoral College results as a fraud.

The influence of the election polls on the decision of the general voting population is verified by the results reported by the media on the night before the 2008 national election, namely 59% of the voters had made up their minds weeks before that Barack Obama would win. Less than a year later in 2009, the same percentage--59%--strongly opposes the programs, actions, and legislative proposals of now President Obama.

A careful review of the results of the election polls of the 2008 election reveals that in spite of everything presented by the liberal media condemning Vice-Presidential Candidate Sarah Palin and her family, she was very popular with the American public and the Republican Party (equally as or ever more popular then the Vice-Presidential Candidate of the Democratic Party among its delegates). The American public {88%} were so tired of the election polls information spread by the media that they were exceedingly happy the election was over and they could return to the regular news of the day. More than half of them felt that the politics in Washington, D.C. would not become more accommodating and helpful than the previous administration: politics as usual among the "good ol` boys club inside the beltway" with their "Fuzzy Ideas From Foggy Bottom" The 111th Congress has certainly proved those American Voters prescient with its total lack of partisanship, oversight, and transparency while spending more money than all Congresses in the previous 222 years combined.

## CHAPTER FIVE

## TWO AMERICAS

The United States of America can be divided into political regions representing various geographic and ethnic areas and including the wealthy, the middle class, and the poor. Divisions to be considered might be as follows: New England, Atlantic, South, Midwest, Rocky Mountain, West(including Hawaii) and Northwest (including Alaska). Encompassed in these areas are the two Americas. What do these two comprise? Democrats versus Republicans--No! Black versus Whites--No! Hispanics versus Anglos--No! In reality, the two Americas are the liberal leftists versus the conservatives. Recent activities at the level of the Federal Government have totally polarized the people of the United States into two groups, one of which wishes to take back control of their country (Tea Party Movement)-- against another camp sympathetic to the liberal Government that is trying to solidify its total power into a base that will be difficult to thwart. The latter camp is engaged in a power grab centered on forcing laws and cultural changes onto the populace , 80% of which is adamantly. opposed!

Should not we remember that all men are  created equal with inalienable rights and that the sovereignity  lies with the people and that no individual nor group shall exercise its control to the contrary. The Founding Fathers hated political parties. It was their contention that quarreling factions (both sides of the aisles in Congress) would be more interested in opposing each other than work-Ing for the common good of the American people. Thusly, one voter-one vote!

The liberal camp seeks power to format change in a covert, insidious manner, whereby the legislative course of action, including activities of the various committees of the U.S. Congress that are conducted behind closed doors. This secrecy prohibits other Members of the Congress representing the opposing political party and their staff from attending as well as instructing them not to speak with the press nor the American people regarding their deliberations without their first prior approval. Enough is enough! The leaders of this practice or political maneuvering principally represent the large metropolitan areas versus large numbers of the Congress who represent mostly rural and suburban areas. This raises the issue once again, of the "Two Americas", only this time it is urban versus rural. It is the return to the Federalist type of government known to the earlier American infant country under the control of Alexander Hamilton. Such power grabbing acts are resulting in the metamorphosis of the American politic together with the alienation of the American voters, who at this time rate the U.S .Congress below 20% approval. This low grade is assigned by all of the electorate , including those claiming to be Democrats, Republicans, and Independents. Again there arises the specter of the "Two Americas" --Populace versus Government. Today, the actions of Congress make a mockery of the 56 Members of the Constitutional Convention who wrote the Bill of Rights, defining the country's governing ideology is that democracy is government answerable to the citizens.

# INDEPENDENTS ASPIRATIONS

Among the political regions of the United States of America described previously, lies the demography of the political parties, Democratic and Republican. Increasingly , however, a sizeable group of voting constituents identifies itself as Independents. A careful review of recent surveys conducted following the election of 2008 reveals that the Democrats represent 72 million voters, compared to the Republicans with 55 million, and the Independents possessing 42 million. Democrats and Republicans spent massive amounts of campaign money courting the Independents, a majority of which voted with the Democrats wishing for the "change" proposed by the Democratic candidate. In so doing, they created a group known as the Obama Independents.

Subsequently, the "change" to which they aspired never happened and at this time are greatly disappointed more with the U.S. Congress than the Presidential candidate they supported. The Independents ought to be looking for another principal source with which to develop a meaningful third political Party. They should forget the method by which development of the two major political parties transpired after the Civil War. There is a fertile field of disappointed members of the two principal parties that could be cultured with the proper direction to join their 42 million, thereby creating a $3^{rd}$ party containing sufficient votes to control every future national election.

Geographically this sizeable group resides in the South and the West regions of the United States. The "blue-blood" Republicans of the New England and Atlantic regions look down on the Republicans of the South and the West as come-again-lately country folks that for hundreds of years were really Democrats and knew nothing about the real values of the Republicans.

At the same time, traditional Democrats of the same New England and Atlantic regions,--for example the Massachusetts Democratic machine run by the Kennedy/Fitzgerald group-- consider the Democrats of the South and the West as an irrelevant newer group of the Party in need of proper political training before their acceptance as equal partners.

Therefore, the Independents might consider approaching and appealing to these two groups outside the expected channels of their respective parties by convening a national organizing convention that would embrace their traditional principles, create a new platform of standards for the new Independent Party and declare to the American public there shall be a significant transformation of the election procedure whereby the electorate will have a choice. A breath of fresh air would be crossing the country, with new aspirations and hopes of the people to have a chance to take back their Government from the special Interest groups and the liberal leftist of the East and West Coasts that now control the Government. " Latter-day Patriots" might be considered their new name. .

# CHAPTER SIX

## BREAKING THE NATIONAL PIGGY BANK... AND YOURS TOO

The addition of 13 trillion dollars to the national debt over the next ten years should scare the collective pants off of responsible Americans. Extremely tough times with the economic situation of 2008- 2009 are devastating the United States of America, while in one year the U.S. Government spent more than all previous U.S. Governments combined. Of the total income for the 2010 Federal Budget, 40 % will be borrowed. Never before has the amount borrowed been more than 20 %. Our Founding Fathers in the Continental Congress took upon themselves the responsibility, authority, and provision of the funds needed to run the infant country, while permitting the Executive Branch to utilize the money according to the laws authorized by the Congress.

The utter downfall of the dollar has ensued in the wake of the recent financial catastrophe, and the calamity has been compounded by the fact that the majority in the U.S. Congress, the House of Representatives as well as the Senate and the Executive Branch are of the same political party. That power has enabled to control both the appropriations and the expenditures of the U.S. Government. To further aggravate the situation , the U.S. Department of the Treasury prints more paper money than the value of the existing gold standard that supposedly backs that paper. This is what happened with the TARP bailout of financial institutions in late 2008,followed by an $800 billion stimulus package, the cap and trade legislation currently under consideration, and the two

versions of the health care reform legislation passed by the House of

Representatives and the Senate in 2009 which with the imminent conciliation in

conference of which is projected to cost $ 3 trillion over the next ten years.

The economic crisis and successive budget crisis have morphed into a debt

calamity of unmanageable proportions. Collusion between the majority of the

members of the U.S. Congress and the Executive Branch has a single purpose:

to effect a socialist agenda.

The United States of America is still a great democracy sustained by the

productivity of individuals whose cumulative efforts and work inform the national

wealth in the hope it will contribute to the well-being of their children and grand-

children. Nevertheless, the financial meltdown we face-- with no escape in

sight---and the predictable high inflation resulting from over-spending and over-

borrowing are projected to cause 30 % devaluation of the dollar in the coming

year. Thomas Jefferson once observed: "When the people fear their government

there is tyranny---when the government fears the people--there is LIBERTY"

Nowadays, special interests with outsized political influence successfully

are peddling their demands and in the process accruing to themselves the

revenues of the U.S. Government. In effect, money is passing from those who

produce to those who do nothing--from host to parasite. Remember the chapter

on lobbyists?

It might be time to create a 28th Amendment to the Constitution that states:

"Congress shall make no law that applies to the citizens of the United States

of America that does not apply equally to the Senators and Representatives

and Congress shall make no law that applies equally to the Senators and

Representatives that does not apply to the citizens of the United States of

America". If we have to pay, then they have to pay, (remember all of those

former Congressmen appointed to jobs in this administration (Obama) who

had forgotten .after all they were too busy, to pay their taxes!

Where do our Federal tax dollars go? The national debt is now at $13 trillion!

When the U.S. Government proposes to spend more money than it takes in as

revenue, individual and corporate taxes, it is called a "budget deficit" When the

deficit balloons up, so do your taxes as special interests arrange for Congress to

create spending programs. That is where your tax dollars are going!

Each year since 1969, the U.S. Congress has spent more money than it has

taken in---taxpayer money. The Department of the Treasury has to borrow

money to meet the appropriations of the Congress. Those Americans who have

recently received benefits as a result of stipulations in the stimulus package

promoted by the Obama administration and approved by Congress believe the

U.S. Government has plenty of money for their pet projects--projects that were

earmarked as amendments to the legislation by their respective Representative

or Senator--legislation none of them read, much less discussed in its entirety!

Those advantaged constituents need to understand that here is no such thing as "Government money!" It is taxpayer money--citizen money! For society as a whole, nothing comes as " right or a claim". One can only have a right to something that has to be produced by forcing someone to produce it. The more the recipients and the greater the distributed (re-distributed) benefit's the producers/providers have to carry the larger the load.

The economic crisis we face today has become a debt crisis. Look at it like a business! If businesses could print money--like the Department of the Treasury does and give it to their customers to buy their products, most folks would shout with joy. However, the business would soon enter bankruptcy! That is exactly where the U.S. Government under the current administration Is headed, with money levied on the taxpayer, taking an ever larger chunk of their paychecks. Every payday working Americans have withdrawn from their paychecks, taxes and donations to the Social Security trust fund. Is your money being spent the way you want it spent?

As pointed out in the previous paragraphs, all Americans will have to pay federal taxes on any and all earned income, including interest or dividends received, and the tax rates on that income are about to shoot up. In addition, although there are deductions--federal tax--each pay period, all working Individuals and those not working, like those living on pensions must file a tax return each year.

Most Americans understand that, according to the Constitution, government income and expenditures should be uniform throughout the United States of America. In reality, however, nothing could be further from the truth! A careful review of Figure 1 on revenue and Figures 2 and 3 reveals there is a disparity between who pays and who benefits. It is estimated that 2 % of the U.S. population pay the taxes, and the rest enjoy the expenditures. Total revenue for the U.S. Government for the fiscal year 2009 was $ 4.636 billion, whereas the national debt exceeded $13 trillion, with more than 40% of that amount borrowed (shown in Figures 2 and 3).Based on these numbers, no matter who you are, your taxes are going to be higher. Taking into consideration the current 10% unemployment in the United States and the projected costs of the health care reform legislation passed by the House of Representatives and in the Senate---soon to be merged into one bill in conference--taxes loaded onto backs of the citizens and their children will become exorbitant and very difficult to pay . as household budgets are completely devastated.

The current U.S. leadership is planning to raise taxes on all corporations, costs that ultimately passed onto the consumers, inevitably will be subsumed in the price of every product they produce. In effect, you the consumer will have to pay these taxes on top of your own.

## FIGURE 1

**Total Budgeted\* Government Revenue**
Revenue GDP — CHARTS — Deficit Debt

| Total | Federal | State | Local |

2009 ▾

Revenue / Pie Chart

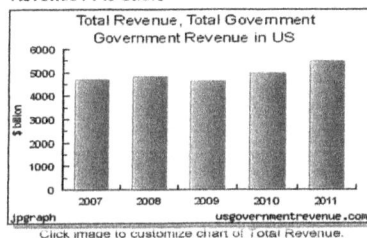 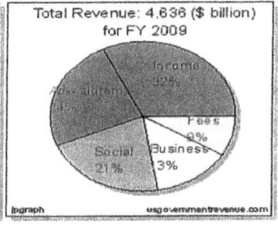

Click image to customize chart of Total Revenue.
For Revenue as %GDP from 1950-2010 click here.

Deficit / Debt

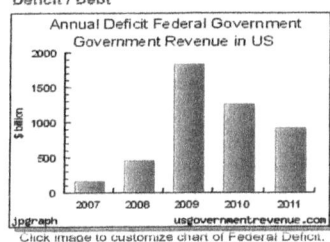 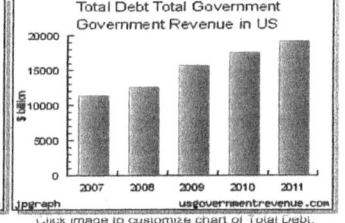

Click image to customize chart of Federal Deficit.
For deficit as %GDP from 1950-2010 click here.

Click image to customize chart of Total Debt.
For debt as %GDP from 1950-2010 click here.

GDP / Revenue by Type

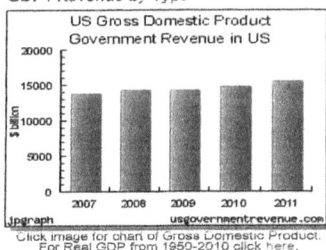

Total Revenue by Type
Values in $ billion
(Click year for details)

| | 2007 | 2008 | 2009 | 2010 | 2011 |
|---|---|---|---|---|---|
| Total Revenue | 33 | 4,840 | 4,636 | | |
| Income Taxes | 884 | | .479 | ,8 | |
| Social Insurance Taxes | 15 | | | | |
| Other Taxes | 18 | 067 | | 151 | |
| Fees and Charges | 36 | 74 | 392 | 426 | |
| Business and Other Revenue | 52 | 74 | | 56 | |

click label above for chart

Note:
\* Federal revenue after 2008 is budgeted. State revenue after 2007 and local revenue after 2006 are "guesstimated."

**FIGURE 2**

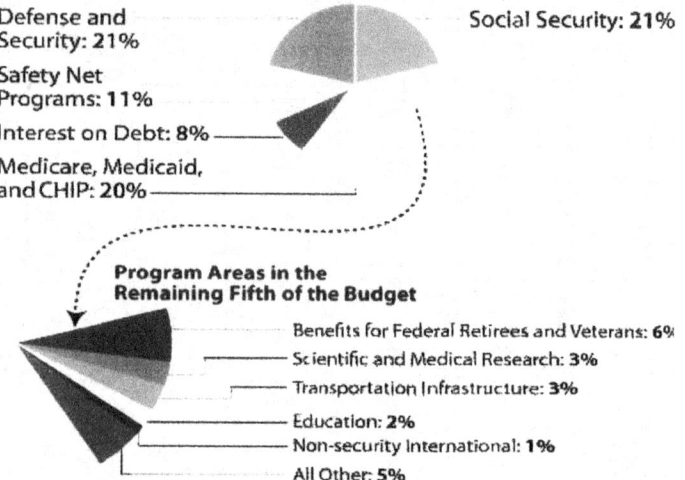

**Most of Budget Goes Toward Defense,
Social Security, and Major Health Programs**

Defense and
Security: 21%

Social Security: 21%

Safety Net
Programs: 11%

Interest on Debt: 8% ———

Medicare, Medicaid,
and CHIP: 20% ——————————

**Program Areas in the
Remaining Fifth of the Budget**

Benefits for Federal Retirees and Veterans: **6%**

Scientific and Medical Research: **3%**

Transportation Infrastructure: **3%**

Education: **2%**

Non-security International: **1%**

All Other: **5%**

Source: Congressional Budget Office
Note: Percentages may not total 100 due to rounding.

# FIGURE 3

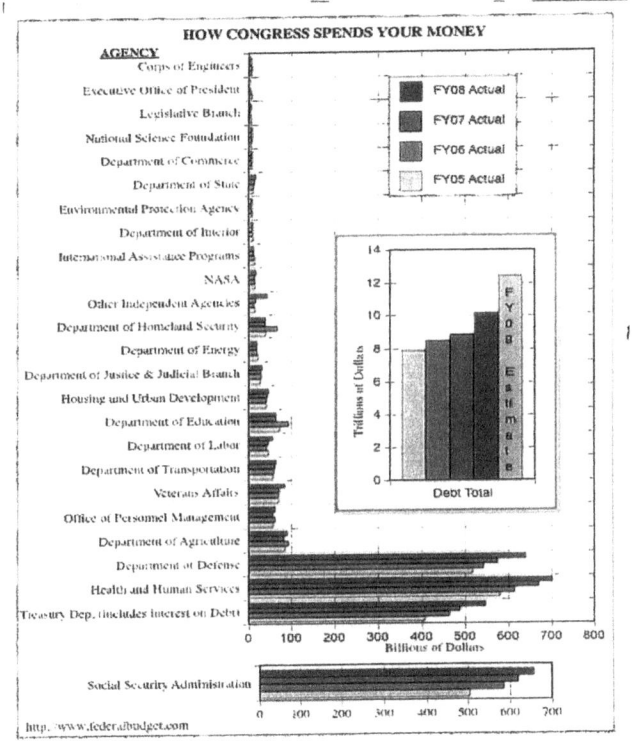

## HOW CONGRESS SPENDS YOUR MONEY

**AGENCY**

Corps of Engineers
Executive Office of President
Legislative Branch
National Science Foundation
Department of Commerce
Department of State
Environmental Protection Agency
Department of Interior
International Assistance Programs
NASA
Other Independent Agencies
Department of Homeland Security
Department of Energy
Department of Justice & Judicial Branch
Housing and Urban Development
Department of Education
Department of Labor
Department of Transportation
Veterans Affairs
Office of Personnel Management
Department of Agriculture
Department of Defense
Health and Human Services
Treasury Dep. (Includes Interest on Debt)

Social Security Administration

FY08 Actual
FY07 Actual
FY06 Actual
FY05 Actual

FY09 Estimate

Debt Total
Trillions of Dollars

Billions of Dollars

http://www.federalbudget.com

# COME PIGGY-GO HOME WITH ME

In the 2008 presidential election, Republican Candidate John McCain
stated "an elaborate influence peddling scheme in which both parties conspire to
stay in office by selling the country to the highest bidder." The Signers of The
Declaration of Independence said , " patriotism has been replaced by greed,
both political and financial." Thus the birth of " pork barrel politics." Let us take
a long look at some prime examples. Firstly, referred by Vice- Presidential
Candidate of the Republican Party in the 2008 election, Governor Sarah Palin
was the "bridge to nowhere" in Alaska, which as Governor she rejected totally.
One more which most Americans know very little about is the federally funded
"Equal Access to Justice Act (EAJA) and the Judgment Fund " which has been
exploited by environmental groups such as the Sierra Club and the Center For
Biodiversity . These groups have been filing lawsuits against the Department of
Agriculture ( National Forest Service) and the Department of the Interior (Bureau
of Land Management) over cattlemen grazing their cattle on federal public
lands. These agencies were using the federal funds of the EAJA to pay lawyers
up to $ 650.00 per hour to prepare and execute the lawsuits. Many times they
filed the lawsuits in Federal Court before notifying the Departments they were
being sued. Correspondingly, the Departments had very little time to prepare
their defense. A bicameral group of members of Congress have requested the
Attorney General and Department of Justice to conduct a thorough review of

this matter . Another occurrence was by a group called Western Watersheds Project , dedicated to ending domestic livestock grazing on federal lands, received nearly a million dollars in reimbursed legal expenses as a result of EAJA.. The EAJA was established by Congress to ensure individuals, small businesses or public interest groups with limited financial resources could seek judicial redress from unreasonable government actions. The EAJA allows prevailing plaintiffs to recover attorney fees and other costs from the federal government itself. Many of the environmental groups have fashioned a virtual litigation industry using this government funded program to bankroll their lawsuits against the federal government by using federal funds.

So there is where your taxpayer money goes!. Spending by the U.S. Government now is totally out of control. U.S. Congress action is like putting a band-aid on a hemorrhage. The U.S. Government does not have the ability to pay off the $11.8 trillion debt . It has too many persons in the decision making process and the execution of programs that functioned very well over the years. In addition, the U.S. Government is excessively large and unmanageable to be successful with many huge programs or social impact . It becomes apparent that the proposed Health Care Reform bill being debated in the U.S. Senate will be unmanageable also. These are all signs of the lack of political knowledge of a weak President and a demanding Congress of the same Party.

# CHAPTER SEVEN

## WHERE THE BUCK STOPS

The cowboy poet/ humorist/ veterinarian Baxter Black, DVM said to me once that the sign "The Buck Stops Here" should set on the desk of each and every President of the United States of America. For truly, with all of the Cabinet Members , Advisors and Czars, some confirmed by the U.S. Senate and some not confirmed, depending upon the importance of their position, the final decisions of the Executive Branch rests totally with the President of the United States of America. Sometimes handling the 'Buck", especially in times of war becomes more difficult the rodeo clown trying to defend the cowboy just bucked off of a 2000 lb bull.

Standing behind the President , in times of difficult decisions are 15 Cabinet members , heads of the 15 different Departments of the Executive Branch and a series of 32 "czars" who serve as advisors tasked with custody of coordination among the various agencies. Some are in charge of specific policy areas for the President. When the President makes a decision very unpopular with the citizens, the President can say that it was based on the advice of the advisors. It is kind of like managing by committee. It is more like elephants breeding! There is a lot of noise; they stir up a lot of dust and it takes 3 yrs to see the results. Significantly, these actions are all conducted oftentimes without participation nor approval by the legislative or judicial branches, of the Government. It appears the "Buck" just gets passed around!

The Departments of the Executive Branch functioning under the authority and responsibility of the President are--Agriculture; Commerce; Defense; Education; Energy; Health and Human Services; Homeland Security; Housing and Urban Development; Justice; Labor; State; Interior; Treasury; Transportation; and Veterans Affairs. The Secretaries, as the heads of these Departments , serve as the Cabinet of the President. In addition, there are Boards, Commissions, Committees, Quasi-Official Agencies and Independent Agencies and Government Corporations. The responsibility for the conduct of some of these is passed into the hands of the Vice-President. All of these appointees are of the same political philosophy of the President and with a majority of the same political party in control of the U.S. Senate, their confirmation is guaranteed.

The U.S. Government today demonstrates the political philosophy toward Socialism , with tendencies of totalitarianism, as demonstrated with some 40 percent of the population already having reached the "governmental dependency" phase. The philosophy of redistribution of the wealth from the 2 % who own most of the wealth to the rest of the population is evidence. The Founding Fathers saw this on the horizon and cemented our inalienable human rights in the Constitution so that all future laws and government actions had to keep these in their thoughts and rulings. The guarantee is the ballot box!

Many Americans would be greatly surprised to learn there are more taxes

by the Federal Government than the income, payroll and social security taxes.

A colossal amount based on each purchase of specific goods such as

cigarettes, gasoline, coal, telephones, tires, gambling and some highway usage

are programmed as excise taxes. The American taxpayer is about to have new

additional payroll taxes subtracted from their pay in the form of a surtax or war

tax to support the war in Afghanistan.

The U.S. Government described in the previous paragraphs moving toward

a socialistic political philosophy enhances a system of taxation on everything in

the daily life of its citizens for the purpose of building a bigger government of

one party and away from the centrist policy upon which the United States of

America flourished since 1850. In this manner, it will be extremely difficult

to remove it from control. The Founding Fathers ( Signers of The Declaration

Of Independence) moved from bondage under the British to a spiritual faith

and from that to great courage, and onto liberty. Subsequently, the 40% of

Americans who have moved to "governmental dependency" have pushed

the country from liberty to abundance. Now the abundance is directing the

United states of America into complacency , then onto apathy and again to

dependence and back in to bondage. Only this time into the hands of a different

demagogue who will be manipulative and dangerous. A significant way to

reform such a government is to decentralize it by cutting off the head of hydra.

## CHAPTER  EIGHT

## SADDLE  UP AND MOVE  `EM  OUT

All of America was knocked to their knees and prayed on the morning of September 11, 2001 when the 2 commercial jet planes crashed deliberately into the twin towers of the World Trade Center. Concurrently, another crashed into The Pentagon , Washington, D.C. further exposing our airspace vulnerability. Thanks to our brave Americans aboard Flt 93, with a target of the White House, they caused it to crash into a rural field in Pennsylvania killing themselves , the hijackers and all passengers. Each aircraft was hijacked by Islamic Jihad terrorists who were trained in the United States of America at various airfields and boarded the aircrafts with valid visas on the East coast utilizing card board cutting knifes as weapons.

The chance that the entire Federal Government could have been completely destroyed was of the highest probability. The last time that happened was during the War Of 1812 by the British trying to recapture the United States Of America. It brought to the attention of the American people how quickly the concentration of the location of the total U.S. Government could be eliminated by 1 great stroke of power. It brought to mind the possibility that those same terrorists might have been carrying a nuclear weapon aboard, like maybe in their luggage. Our Trust In God was fortified that day when we were spared such a catastrophic  holocaust ! The remedy and solution to this vulnerability  and concentration of authority/responsibility is decentralization of the Government.

## DECENTRALIZATION

A very significant question most Americans might ask could be," Why shift an important political government unit from a position at the top to a lesser significant location?" The basic theory behind decentralization is to move all Departments of the Executive Branch , with the exception of the Department Of Defense, Department of Homeland Security, Department of Justice and the Department of State, away from the Washington D.C. metropolitan area to the interior of the United States of America. The most important but obvious rationale for affecting the move is to ensure, maybe guarantee, a more secure environment from which the Departments may continue to function away from possible terrorist activity. Furthermore, the metropolitan area of Washington, DC Is more difficult to defend than cities scattered across the Country. The airspace there is extremely vulnerable, like New York City, as exemplified by the flyover of the aircraft authorized by the White House to take photographs and scared the hundreds of thousands of New Yorkers once again.

Moreover, The U.S. Government operates at the highest level of modern electronic communication today with immediate contact among the Departments of the Executive Branch within seconds. Likewise, rapid aircraft transportation among all cities with thousands of flights daily ensures movement of personnel at a moments notice , if necessary. Additional benefit would be less automobile Traffic in the Washington, D.C. metropolitan area and less persons in danger.

Why would persons in the seat of the U.S. Government be in more danger In Washington, D.C. than say Denver ,Colorado? Let us suppose a terrorist placed a nuclear device on board an Amtrak Train , either as carry-on luggage or placed on the undercarriage of a train car. Should the device be detonated on arrival at Union Station, the U.S. Congress, and the Supreme Court ,would disintegrate instantly and the rest of Washington, D.C. would follow , including Northern Virginia and the Maryland suburbs. More importantly , there would be no early warning with which to prepare. Such a catastrophic holocaust would make the World Trade Center appear minimal.

Equally important in the movement of the Departments into the interior of the Country would be the significant economic impact on the recipient States and their cities and surrounding areas. Many States are functioning today in deficit spending, such as Arizona, California and Michigan and an infusion of the magnitude of the money brought by a Department of the Executive Branch would resolve their budget woes. Additionally, it would assist in relief of the status of unemployment.

The proposition recommending the decentralization will meet with what might appear to be insurmountable and great obstacles such as opposition from the entrenched professional politicians with their lawyer titles. To placate these politicians, continue the Secretary of each Department in Washington, D.C.

What are the parameters for relocation and how much of the

U.S. Government would be moved to principal cities of various States?

There is no essential rationale for maintaining parts of the various departments

of the Executive Branch in Washington, D.C. when there are economic, security

and political benefits to be achieved in the States.

Efforts by all Americans will be needed to convince Congress to amend

The Constitution , which may be legally crucial to implementing such moves.

Should Congress refuse to assist with the suggestion, the voting populace could

place propositions on the ballots in every State during the national elections

authorizing their Senators to vote for the amendment.

The relocation process could be as follows:

1) Department of Agriculture> Omaha, Nebraska

2) Department of Commerce> St. Louis, Missouri

3) Department of Education> Harrisburg, Pennsylvania

4) Department of Energy> Denver, Colorado

5) Department of Health and Human Services> Atlanta, Georgia

6) Department of Housing and Urban Development>Nashville, Tenn.

7) Department of Labor> Detroit, Michigan

8) Department of Interior> Sacramento, California

9) Department of Transportation> Dallas, Texas

10) Department of Veterans Affairs> Phoenix, Arizona

## CHAPTER NINE

## STAND UP AMERICA

It is a basic principle of management that to bring about behavior changes within a corporation or other business, it is essential to first bring about changes in mental attitude. Most often, it is more difficult to acquire the mental adjustments than the behavior changes that follow.. For instance, the American public has requested the U.S. Congress, over many years, to make pending legislation available on the internet so that perusal is accessible. The secretcy by the Democrat leadership in the U.S. Senate with the Health Care Reform Bill is a prime example of the lack of behavior changes entrenched in the professional politicians. Huge changes are essential for the American public to regain control of their government as well as the taxpayer's money.

Sometimes it calls upon a generation to be great and that generation Is now ! Let us bring together " The Greatest Generation" with the " Newer Generation" whereby all stand up and speak up with positive proposals to bring about changes..Such activities will return our Democracy to the hands of the people of all generations now and to come.

"The Hope still lives and the Dream shall never die!" ( John F. Kennedy) STAND UP AMERICA AND SPEAK UP! LET FREEDOM RING IN YOUR VOICES AS THEY ARE HEARD FROM EVERY MOUNTAIN TOP FROM SEA TO SHINING SEA! GOD BLESS AMERICA!

# ABOUT THE AUTHOR

Harold B. Hubbard lives in Hereford, Arizona with his Golden Retriever,

Skooter. He was raised in rural Central Ohio; graduated from Jacksontown High

School, Jacksontown, Ohio; served 31/2 years in the U.S. Navy Air Corps near

the end of WWII; graduated from The Ohio State University with Doctor of

Veterinary Medicine; graduated from The University of California (Berkeley) with

Masters in Public Health. Served as Associate Professor (Epidemiology) in The

University of Georgia; Dr. Hubbard served 16 years as a Senior Staff Officer

with The Pan American Health Organization. He practiced private and public

veterinary medicine for 55 years. He studied American politics all of his life,

understanding the scheme of the politician's agenda, using the indoctrination

from his Democratic Party father. Most of the contents of this book emanated

from expression of his thoughts on politics to his family and friends who insisted

he write about them.

www.ingramcontent.com/pod-product-compliance
Lightning Source LLC
Chambersburg PA
CBHW060647290526
45793CB00001B/433